AFRICA DAY IN THE UNITED KINGDOM: A MODERN PERSPECTIVE, IN CONJUNCTION WITH THE SOUTH AFRICAN ASSOCIATION SAAN

The book is a jubilant celebration of African culture, featuring a captivating collection of photographs that showcase various aspects of multicultural life in Swindon, a vibrant town in the UK. Among these images are moments captured with the South African Minister of Sport at the historic City Hall of Pietermaritzburg and heartwarming scenes from an African community gathering held in one of Swindon's lush parks. Additionally, it includes a snapshot of a renowned UK television contestant dancer from the popular program, "Guess His Name," aired on the Blue Sky network, as part of Activity One.

The net profits generated from this book will be dedicated to supporting the invaluable work of the South African Association (SAAn). This modern narrative of Africa is a testament to the power of unity, aiming to foster a sense of togetherness among the continent's diverse populations and engage people worldwide in meaningful endeavours. The project was a collaborative effort utilising platform like Facebook, WhatsApp, various social media channels, and community events, encouraging individuals to share their photos, messages, and interviews. This initiative was a powerful means of crafting a fresh and inspiring story of Africa, highlighting its rich culture and the potential for collective achievements.

"Living in contemporary Africa and the United Kingdom, we experience a rich blend of ancient civilisations and modern complexities that captivates and engages us." South African Association Chairperson Cllr Bazil Solomon describes his journey from South African schooling to living and working in the UK and looking after communities in Swindon, UK, to South Africa Pietermaritzburg

With great Western heritage and Zulu musical talent, Johnny Clegg and Savuka took the stage, joined by the Honourable Nelson Mandela. Standing tall in a striking African shirt, Mandela declared, "Music and dancing bring me peace with the world and within myself. However, I want to see more movement back there! Let's get everyone to join in!"

I love seeing children and young people enjoying outdoor life, which is essential for our young children. Play is the foundation of learning, creativity, self-expression, and constructive problem-solving. It's how children wrestle with life to make it meaningful": Fatima Whitbread OBE, who is running a campaign to help children have good quality family life no matter their circumstances.

"In our lifetime end child poverty": Nic Careem, who runs the Sign the Nelson Mandela Book Project, brings people worldwide together.

CONTENTS

CHAPTER 1:
INTRODUCTION

Dear Reader, we invite you to embark on an inspiring journey that takes you from the charming town of Swindon in the United Kingdom to Africa's vibrant, bustling cities. Our aim is to create a rich tapestry of interviews that showcase personal stories from these locales, stories that will resonate with you and enhance your understanding of the African culture. These stories are enhanced by captivating photographs highlighting everyday individuals alongside renowned personalities and significant events. Get ready for an engaging adventure: can you guess their names and locations?

Our narrative for Africa Day goes beyond mere exploration of landscapes and cultures; it celebrates the brilliant students we meet in classrooms filled with eager minds around the globe. To ensure anonymity, all names have been changed; if any name sounds familiar, please rest assured that it is purely coincidental.

As Dieter, a well-liked student on campus who often quotes the Magna Carta, the Equalities Act, South Africa's Constitution, and human rights bills, highlights, inclusion is a key focus in the UK and Africa. Dieter aspires to become a lawyer and works tirelessly on community projects to gain admission to Oxford University.

Our journey includes photographs from an award ceremony for community work in football, featuring a visit to Number 10 Downing Street, where we met the Minister of Sport and other figures instrumental in sports across the UK. Community photographer Kristy was present. Sharon, Charmaine, and Nana captured moments with members of the Zulu heritage community in Wimbledon, London, during South African Heritage Day with DAAbroadUK, and they attended events with South African ministers at the Liberal Club in Whitehall. Additionally, Sharon was privileged to meet Dr Saths Cooper at his Oxford University Union talks and promote rugby in Swindon. Saths served as a political prisoner in Robin Island with Nelson Mandela. Saths is from the author's wife's family. The author's family served and currently serves as MPs, Councillors and Mayors, bringing people together through good times and tough times to succeed.

Throughout this journey, we recognise the numerous challenges faced by people from Africa across the globe. From the rich music of the Caribbean, with legends like Bob Marley and Rihanna, to the historical struggles around Windrush issues, colonisation, and slavery, many nations from Europe to Africa share intertwined histories. Yet, amid the trials, modern African cities are filled with advocates for peace and prosperity. Let's never give up, never give in, and ensure that the flame of ambition and talent within millions of African heritage youth continues to burn bright, guiding them towards a future of significant progress.

"Wherever you are in the world, the yearning for belonging is deeply felt. At different points in our lives, we all encounter the feeling of being a minority." Jasmine, lost in her thoughts, slowly raised her hand, her long arms stretching toward the sky. When she finally spoke, her words resonated throughout the classroom, capturing the attention of her classmates, who sat up straight, intrigued by her perspective.

This book is dedicated to the beloved individuals who have shaped our communities and have since passed away, leaving behind a treasure trove of wisdom. We hope to spark your curiosity and encourage you to dive deeper into the rich tapestry of Africa, inspiring discussions with fellow students, teachers, lecturers, family, and friends about our shared journey.

"You have countless career paths ready for you to explore:

from the arts of acting and drama to the rhythm of music, from the practical skills offered by electrician apprenticeships to the dynamic fields of IT and artificial intelligence. Consider programming, medicine, law, administration, entrepreneurship, and sports like football and netball. There's a place for those interested in policing, politics, culinary arts, nursing, teaching, travel writing, diplomacy, and even train driving. With unwavering support from one another, you will accomplish remarkable things that go beyond your current circumstances," passionately proclaimed the experienced lecturer in Jasmine's college class as he moved confidently around the room, his enthusiasm infectious.

We are wholeheartedly committed to supporting and nurturing our communities, striving to connect with people from all different backgrounds. This book is dedicated to our wonderful South African friend, Vishen, whose talents as an event organiser and party planner brought joy and unity to countless gatherings. In his memory, we held a heartfelt vigil service at Holy Rood Church in Swindon, where friends and loved ones came together to celebrate his life and his lasting impact on us all.

Question Time: What specific experiences shaped Jasmine's insights on belonging? How did excellent skills as an event organiser impact the communities served? What legacy of wisdom do the individuals honoured in the dedication leave for future generations?

Carstens: "A significant and transformative moment for me was when Archbishop Desmond Tutu visited us. His heartfelt speech left a lasting impression on us as students and provided an invaluable education. Additionally, I can't forget the annual Comrades Marathon, which winds through Kloof. Each year, it's a truly inspiring experience to witness people from all walks of life supporting each other during the gruelling 84-kilometre race under the scorching sun."

ACTIVITY 1: I encourage you to work with your lecturer to identify the other notable figures who accompanied the author. Throughout history, both Africa and the UK have seen many remarkable leaders with intertwined legacies, including Nelson Mandela, Helen Zille, Shaka, Fatima Meer, Steve Biko, Jay Naidoo, Sats Cooper, Pops Chetty, Mergen Chetty, Sylvia Solomon, Zayn Adams, Winston Churchill, Margaret Thatcher, Nye Bevan, Stanley Baldwin, Gandhi, Mary Seacole, Harold Moody, Ben Key, and Freddie Mercury.

CHAPTER 2: HISTORY AND MANY HERITAGES IN SWINDON AND AFRICA

Africa's diverse landscapes are home to countless individuals, each with unique stories that blend into the continent's rich history. The San and Khoi peoples have deep roots and have thrived for thousands of years in South Africa's sun-drenched Cape Province. Their vibrant culture, supported by the South African government, continues to be celebrated and preserved, ensuring their heritage lives on.

Over the centuries, Africa has witnessed significant migrations and expansions, particularly with the movements of Arabs and Europeans. The Bantu people embarked on a remarkable journey, migrating from the heart of Upper Africa down to the lush landscapes of KwaZulu-Natal. The Zulu people, known for their courage, fiercely resisted Dutch and British colonisers, and today, they maintain a strong identity under their king while promoting a vibrant cultural legacy.

South Africa's demographic landscape is equally rich, boasting around two million people of British, Dutch (Afrikaner), and Indian descent, alongside a mix of other ethnicities. Within the continent's multitude of identities, we find the Sotho and Xhosa in South Africa, Kikuyu in Kenya, Hausa, Yoruba, and Igbo in Nigeria, and Akan in Ghana, each adding to the beautiful mosaic of African culture.

"In Africa, we believe that while nation-states are undeniably important, open borders—similar to the EU—hold tremendous value," Ashantee passionately emphasised. Surrounded by friends at a lively canteen table, they dove into their studies, flipping through well-worn Royal Mail post-preparation books while their laughter mingled with clinking bottles. Ashantee, with her captivating brown eyes and roots in Ghana but born in Swindon, enjoyed a warm ginger-based drink. The eclectic group included a stylish English woman with trendy glasses, a graceful Goan woman with flowing black hair, and Sade-Amy, who reminisced about her vibrant childhood in Nigeria as DJ Black Coffee's pulsating beats played from BBC Radio 1.

Jambo, Sawabona!

Activity Two: How Many African Languages Can You Greet In?

The South African Association is wholeheartedly committed to celebrating community events, from birthdays and weddings to traditional braai gatherings that bring family and friends together over delicious meals. Our team actively collaborates with community leaders and diverse organisations to maximise our impact, hosting events and participating in high-profile events such as the MTM Awards, which honour excellence in various fields, and MTM Swahili Day at the House of Lords, celebrating the rich heritage of Swahili speakers.

We also work closely with elderly residential homes to ensure our seniors feel appreciated and included in our celebrations. Promoting community involvement is key, and we capture the incredible moments that highlight joy and connection through stunning photographs taken by our talented photographers. Join us in this lively celebration of culture and community!

Some Discussion Topics to Consider:

1. How would you respond to those who argue that emphasising open borders might overlook Africa's complex political and economic challenges today?

2. What are your thoughts on the idea that cultural preservation efforts could be undermined by globalization, potentially diluting traditional practices instead of enhancing them?

3. Have you considered the argument that while diverse ethnic identities enrich Africa, they can also lead to conflicts and divisions among communities?

.

CHAPTER 3: DURBAN, A GREAT SEASIDE CITY IN SOUTH AFRICA

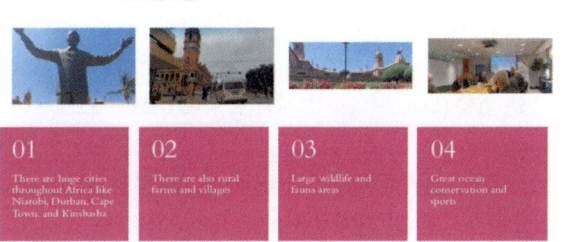

DURBAN A GREAT CITY IN SOUTH AFRICA

01 There are huge cities throughout Africa like Niarobi, Durban, Cape Town, and Kinshasha

02 There are also rural farms and villages

03 Large wildlife and fauna areas

04 Great ocean conservation and sports

Juma from Kenya walked purposefully down a bustling street in Pietermaritzburg, KwaZulu-Natal, South Africa, his feet kicking up loose stones that rattled against the pavement. The lively sounds around him faded momentarily as Jerome's urgent voice pierced the air: "Watch where you're going and stay vigilant; watch out for muggers and car hijackers."

Filled with unwavering resolve, Juma replied, "I stand for law and order and will not put up with lawlessness!" His voice rang with conviction, reflecting the strong principles he held dear. Just days prior, they had enjoyed the vibrant city of Durban, and the allure of Umhlanga had captured their hearts—its stunning beachfront, high-end restaurants, and elegant hotels made it feel like a slice of Europe nestled in South Africa, bustling with holidaymakers soaking up the sun and surf.

Jerome, whose mixed Dutch and San heritage was evident in his beautifully braided hair, walked alongside Juma, both men united by their aspirations for a better future in South Africa. Juma regarded Nairobi, Kenya, as the greatest city on earth, a dynamic hub bursting with opportunities. He had founded a successful tech company there, which was home to many innovative FinTech startups. He treasured the expansive, leafy public parks that provided a serene retreat from the city's frenetic pace.

As a dedicated Pan-African, Juma was passionate about the potential of Africa's youth to reshape the continent and the world for the better. He voiced his strong opposition to wars that cause devastation, such as the conflict between Ukraine and Russia, which had forced many Ukrainian students to seek refuge in places like Swindon. He wanted peace in the middle east, refugees treated with dignity by stronger government initiatives to control borders, he wanted people to get along. During a visit to friends in Bristol, he witnessed the inspiring collaboration among Somali, Polish, and Southern African communities as they rallied to support Ukrainian and Afghan refugees, creating a network of compassion and assistance.

Juma's impactful contributions to ethnic minority work have not gone unnoticed; he has received numerous awards, including a prestigious business accolade that underscores his dedication and significant contributions to these causes.

To explore Juma's journey further, consider these intriguing research avenues:

1. Analyze the context of Juma's journey and the societal challenges he faces in Pietermaritzburg.

2. Research the prevalence and impact of crime in urban South African settings, especially Pietermaritzburg.

3. Investigate the concept of law and order within South Africa's socio-political landscape.

4. Explore the significance of Juma's character traits, such as determination and commitment to Pan-Africanism.

5. Examine Juma's background in Nairobi, focusing on the tech sector and its role in shaping economic opportunities in Africa.

6. Assess the impact of conflicts, like the Ukraine-Russia war, on global migration trends and community solidarity.

7. Gather information on organizations and initiatives that support refugees in the UK, especially concerning ethnic minorities.

8. Look into Juma's recognition and awards to understand his influence in the business and social realms.

9. Consider the cultural dynamics among the various highlighted communities (Somali, Polish, Southern African) and their joint efforts toward common humanitarian goals.

10. Synthesize research findings to craft a cohesive narrative that reflects Juma's ideals and experiences, highlighting themes of unity, resilience, and civic responsibility.

CHAPTER 4: THE POLITICS OF AFRICAN FOODS?

Delving into the intricate relationship between food and African politics reveals a vibrant tapestry woven from culture, history, and identity. This connection is significant and multifaceted, much like the one found in Great Britain. Picture, for instance, a Labour socialist, a passionate advocate for the rights of British miners, who nostalgically recalls the warm, flaky pastries and frothy pints of beer that fostered a sense of camaraderie and solidarity among labourers during their arduous struggles. These culinary comforts were not merely sustenance; they represented resilience and community spirit forged in the heat of shared hardship. Conversely, the Conservative elite finds pleasure in the exquisite flavours of the countryside, often indulging in game dishes crafted from locally sourced ingredients, such as the tender meat of pheasant and the hearty richness of venison. Each meal for them carries an air of tradition and legacy, connecting them to a history of landownership and cultivation. Meanwhile, charismatic leaders of the reform party take to national television, confidently showcasing their appreciation for traditional British ale, symbolizing a nostalgic link to national heritage and a celebration of local brewing artistry.

South Africa's culinary landscape offers a vivid and compelling story of diversity and adaptation that reflects the nation's complex socio-political fabric. Take, for instance, bunny chow— a vibrant and flavorful curry encased in a hollowed-out loaf of bread. This iconic dish was ingeniously developed by indentured Indian labourers who brought their culinary traditions from the subcontinent, integrating them into the local cuisine to create something uniquely South African. Simultaneously, the Afrikaner population, with its Dutch roots, has made significant culinary contributions by introducing beloved delicacies such as biltong, a meticulously cured and spiced meat that has become a staple snack, and boerewors, a sausage infused with a blend of spices that yields a robust flavour profile. Additionally, traditional African lamb stew served with mealie meal bread embodies the essence of communal dining, warming the spirit and bringing people together at the table, showcasing the importance of food in fostering relationships.

The author delights in the vibrant world of cooking, particularly aromatic Durban chicken biryanis, where basmati rice dances harmoniously with spices like cardamom and cinnamon, creating an enticingly fragrant dish. Picture the rich, velvety texture of vegetable curries, featuring succulent pieces of aubergine simmered in a blend of spices that awaken the senses and make your stomach rumble with anticipation.

As dusk falls, the allure of outdoor potjie kos draws family and friends together. This traditional South African stew, cooked slowly in a cast-iron pot over an open flame, infuses the air with warmth while stories and laughter mingle in the glow of the fire, creating a tapestry of cherished memories.

In many African homes, the braai or barbecue serves as a focal point for gatherings, where the tantalizing aroma of grilling meats fills the air. Imagine the sight of glistening fish, plump boerewors coils, thick, juicy T-bone steaks, and tender mutton chops sizzling on the grill, alongside skewers of chicken sosaties marinated in a sweet and savory blend. For vegetarians, the feast is equally enticing, showcasing beloved snacks like biltong and niknaks and heartwarming dishes such as creamy maize porridge and colourful Ethiopian curries, each brimming with fresh, local produce that tells the story of the land.

To complement these culinary delights, guests can enjoy refreshing Coca-Cola, a variety of exquisite African wines like the bold and fruity Pinotage, and smooth, rich Shiraz, alongside cold beers such as Carling and a selection of fine whiskies. The table is also graced with classic Western dishes like a hearty British roast and rich Irish stew, crafting a culinary experience that reflects the rich diversity of flavours, cultures, and traditions that make this gathering a true celebration of community and togetherness.

The political landscape of South Africa is equally colourful and multifaceted, as various parties strive to represent the interests of specific ethnic minorities while competing for influence and power. Each political party navigates a rich tapestry of ideologies; some are committed to democratic principles, advocating for social justice and equality, while others lean toward liberal, conservative, or socialist perspectives, reflecting the country's historical and cultural complexities. This ideological diversity complicates the democratic landscape, prompting ongoing debates on how best to address the needs and aspirations of all South Africans.

The roles of food and music in this context transcend mere entertainment; they function as powerful universal languages of unity and resistance. This was starkly apparent when Nelson Mandela, embodying the spirit of reconciliation and togetherness, shared the stage with celebrated musicians Johnny Clegg and

Savuka during a vibrant concert. With infectious enthusiasm, Mandela rallied the audience, urging them, "I don't see lots of people dancing in the back; let's replay the song 'Asimbonanga' and get more people up and dancing." Such moments are deeply rooted in history—songs like "Give Me Hope, Joanna" were once silenced during the oppressive apartheid regime, a dark chapter where Mandela himself faced unjust imprisonment for his unwavering beliefs and fight for justice.

South Africa's remarkable transition to democracy is celebrated for its unprecedented peacefulness, providing a hopeful vision for a new era for all citizens. Yet, three decades after this monumental shift, the nation stands at a crossroads, confronting serious challenges that threaten its progress: rampant corruption, increasing crime rates, and persistent economic inequalities. It is crucial to rekindle hope, not only to navigate these pressing issues effectively but also to cultivate a prosperous future for all South Africans. This endeavour is vital to ensuring that the spirit of resilience, unity, and collective identity continues to flourish, celebrating the rich cultural heritage that has shaped the nation and its people.

Activity three: can you talk about the African foods you have tried?

AFRICAN FOODS

- Maize meal products
- Biltong
- Ethopian stews
- South African curries
- Carribean pies

CHAPTER 5: SCHOOLS AND UNIVERSITIES WE ATTENDED IN AFRICA & UK

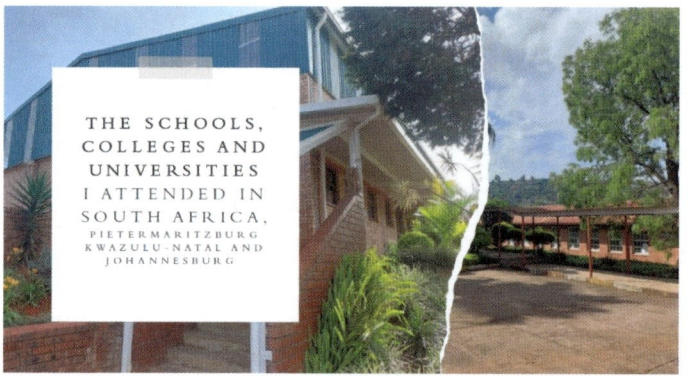

THE SCHOOLS, COLLEGES AND UNIVERSITIES I ATTENDED IN SOUTH AFRICA, PIETERMARITZBURG KWAZULU-NATAL AND JOHANNESBURG

The author recalls a fulfilling educational journey through several esteemed institutions in South Africa, especially the University of Witwatersrand and UNISA. "I have vivid memories of my walks to school, roaming across vast grasslands sprinkled with wildflowers and wandering alongside glistening rivers. I would often pause, captivated by swallows diligently building their intricate mud nests. It's important to note, though, that the education system during my time was far from inclusive. It mainly served children from well-off families who cruised through their studies, largely insulated from the social struggles others faced, wrapped in an atmosphere that provided them with safety and security. While I hold no grudges against the wealthy, I was fortunate to have insightful educators who genuinely believed in my potential and inspired me to aim high."

"Today, I proudly declare that my greatest achievements are rooted in my loving wife and family. I am deeply dedicated to supporting our community, both in good times and bad. My quest for knowledge didn't end there; I pursued further studies at Sunderland University after enrolling through Swindon College, then earned my Post Graduate Certificate in Education (PGCE) from Bath Spa University, and finally completed a research degree at Oxford Brookes University focused on Artificial Intelligence and Linguistics. Throughout this journey, I balanced my studies with full-time work while securing scholarships, proving that determination and hard work can pave the way to success."

"In Africa, countless individuals continue to grapple with access to education. Thankfully, numerous charities are stepping up to provide essential support. The stark contrast between extreme wealth and poverty is unmistakable. In the UK, students frequently face the heavy burden of financing their education through colleges, apprenticeships, and universities, heavily relying on student loans. The current cost of living crisis is affecting families in Swindon and beyond. Connecting with organisations like the Samaritans, Food Collective, and Citizens Advice is crucial, as it offers vital help for mental health issues, debt management, and food security. Don't hesitate to contact your local councillors, MPs, and councils for additional assistance. Educational institutions are also important resources, and the National Union of Students is ready to offer support."

Swindon boasts a fantastic inclusive language guidebook. Carstens, who studied in South Africa years ago, shares: "I finally made my dream come true by returning to Durban, South Africa, to start university there. It was a tough journey, but I succeeded in earning my B.Com. Durban and the university were truly magical places. I was thrilled to make friends from diverse communities, some politically engaged. The learning curve was steep— we witnessed Black Panthers, UDF, Progressives, Conservatives, demonstrations, and public meetings. I got married to my dear partner."

"Never shy away from asking for help during difficult times, and make it a point to recognise and celebrate your achievements, no matter how small. Take it one day at a time. When you need a spark of inspiration or an escape, dive into the music of artists like Lana Del Rey, Djo Cat, Dizzee Rascal, and The Beatles, or soak in the electrifying energy of Heavy Metal," Emma, a proud Scottish LGBTQ+ community leader and student from Lawn Manor, passionately expressed in a local newspaper.

Here are some relevant topics for your current and future studies:

1. Research the history and significance of the University of Witwatersrand and UNISA in South Africa's educational framework.

2. Explore the socio-economic influences affecting access to education in South Africa during the author's school years.

3. Investigate how socioeconomic status impacts educational opportunities and outcomes in South Africa and the UK.

4. Study the role of community charities and organisations addressing educational inequalities in Africa.

5. Analyze the effects of student loans and the financial burdens of education in the UK, especially amid the ongoing cost of living crisis.

6. Examine the support systems in place for students dealing with mental health challenges, debt, and food insecurity in the UK.

7. Investigate the contributions of the National Union of Students and local organisations in supporting students' needs.

8. Review literature on the significance of mentorship and supportive educators in nurturing potential among students from disadvantaged backgrounds.

9. Gather quotes and insights from Emma regarding her experiences and perspectives on education and community support.

10. Create a playlist featuring the music mentioned that can inspire and emotionally uplift students.

CHAPTER 6: AFRICAN COLLEGES, UNIVERSITIES AND COMMUNITY WORK

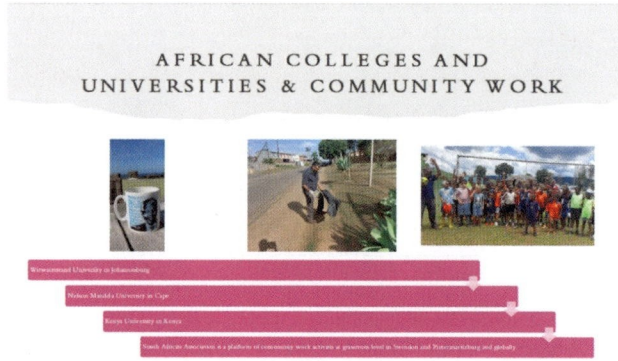

Think!

What specific criteria are used in the Times Higher Education World University Rankings?

How do the universities in South Africa compare to those in Egypt and Algeria regarding academic performance and research output?

What programs or initiatives are in place to enhance higher education across the African continent?

Khumalo argues, "The African continent is rich with a diverse array of colleges and universities, each uniquely contributing to the academic landscape. According to the Times Higher Education World University Rankings 2025, the finest institutions span an impressive 19 countries, showcasing the continent's educational breadth. Uganda stands out in the east, while Nigeria makes its mark to the west. To the north, Morocco shines, and at the southernmost tip, South Africa emerges as a leader in higher education."

In this prestigious ranking, Egypt and Algeria stand out as the two countries with the most universities represented, boasting 35 and 26 institutions, respectively. Remarkably, South Africa dominates the rankings, filling half the top 10 slots and featuring 14 universities. This highlights South Africa's significant role in fostering academic excellence.

Table from https://www.timeshighereducation.com/student/best-universities/best-universities-africa

The South African Association is making considerable strides in promoting impactful grassroots projects that address pressing community needs. Our platform strongly advocates these essential initiatives, particularly emphasising collaboration and community engagement.

In Swindon, we are actively partnering with neighbourhood police watches to tackle knife crime and confront the challenges associated with county-line gang activity, which has become increasingly concerning in urban environments. This collaboration aims to create safer neighbourhoods through community vigilance and support.

Moreover, our unwavering commitment to community well-being is showcased in our ongoing efforts to ensure the continued operation of local libraries and community centres. These spaces are vital resources for residents, providing educational and social opportunities that benefit everyone.

We also recognise the importance of local football and boxing clubs, which are crucial in promoting physical health, teamwork, and youth engagement. In addition to tuition assistance for students, we offer various resources and support to help these clubs thrive, ensuring that individuals from all backgrounds have access to quality education and opportunities.

Suraya: talked about her work. "Hi Stan, here are some of the activities that I'm involved in in South Africa together with my colleagues are:

1. I'm part of many different organisations, like the DA Women's Network, where we deal with issues like gender-based violence, family issues like unemployment and poverty, and the collection and distribution of sanitary pads. I also assist people in finding jobs through networking with other big companies, screening people, and ensuring that the right people are employed.

I also assist old people with filling out forms for Applying for indigent support and other things.

2. We also help with feeding schemes to collect and distribute food to needy people.

3. We have youngsters who also help organise sporting activities in the community and purchase equipment for athletes.

4. I have many ladies' groups where I try to give advice and assistance to people in need and send out important messages to help them. I have a good response from those groups, as women no longer feel alone.

I try to help wherever possible, such as with tuition and sales."

Through these initiatives, the South African Association embodies a comprehensive approach to building community resilience and enhancing the quality of life for all residents.

CHAPTER 7: JOBS AND CAREERS IN AFRICA AND FAMOUS PEOPLE

Saffa was delivering a public talk on his journey as a chef, reaching out to audiences on a TV food channel in Zimbabwe. He emphasised, "Renowned chefs from around the globe craft exceptional menus that showcase the incredible and diverse flavours of the African continent. African cuisine is varied and deeply rooted in its rich agricultural heritage. It represents a dynamic fusion of Indigenous ingredients—think millet, sorghum, and cassava—often paired with culinary techniques and flavours woven through centuries of trade and migration. Iconic dishes like jollof rice—a savoury rice dish generally prepared with tomatoes, onions, and spices—fufu, a starchy accompaniment made from boiled and pounded plantains or yams, and couscous, a staple rooted in North African cultures, exemplify this rich tapestry of culinary artistry."

Paul, an Englishman from Swindon, reminisces about his trips to Africa: "Africa is a land of breathtaking natural wonders, like the magnificent Victoria Falls, one of the largest and most famous waterfalls in the world, and Mount Kilimanjaro, the continent's highest peak, drawing adventurers and nature lovers from far and wide. It's also home to exotic wildlife, including the Big Five—lion, elephant, buffalo, leopard, and rhinoceros—making it a prime destination for ecotourism."

Sarah, who comes from a mixed heritage, shares her experiences and volunteer work: "Africa is a vibrant mosaic of cultural diversity, boasting 56 sovereign states and approximately 1,500 to 2,000 spoken languages. It invites everyone to explore its myriad cultures, traditions, and histories."

International job agencies highlight the continent's career prospects: "Beyond its natural beauty and cultural appeal, Africa has emerged as an attractive hub for business. Notable multinational companies, such as Barclays, Deloitte, DHL, PwC, and Microsoft, have set up significant operational bases across the continent. This growing presence opens remarkable opportunities for professionals looking to advance their careers in a rapidly changing market without switching employers or relocating outside Africa."

Carstens reflects, "In 1988, I began my journey at Standard Bank in Johannesburg as a Management Trainee. I made many new friends from diverse backgrounds and was trained across various sectors, including the exciting world of the Foreign Exchange Dealing Room and International Finance. Eventually, I became a foreign trade consultant at the International Service Centre, which I believe stemmed from my European trading background.

Colleges note: "Studying abroad in Africa offers an extraordinary chance to immerse oneself in this dynamic environment. The continent is home to 41 universities that consistently achieve recognition for their academic excellence, featuring prominently in the QS World University Rankings 2024. These institutions provide a variety of programs and opportunities to engage with a lively student community, making the experience both educational and transformative."

Group Tasks:

1. Research the diversity of African cuisine and its regional variations throughout the continent.

2. Identify key Indigenous ingredients commonly used in African cooking, such as millet, sorghum, and cassava.

3. Explore the historical influences on African cuisine, mainly how trade and migration have shaped cooking techniques and flavours.

4. Investigate iconic African dishes like jollof rice, fufu, and couscous, detailing their origins, preparation methods, and cultural significance.

5. Examine the role of renowned chefs in promoting African cuisine globally, highlighting their contributions to culinary innovation and menu development.

6. Gather information about Africa's natural wonders, including Victoria Falls and Mount Kilimanjaro, and discuss their impact on tourism and cultural appreciation.

7. Research the Big Five wildlife and their importance in ecotourism, emphasising conservation efforts and their effects on local economies.

8. Analyze the presence of multinational corporations in Africa and the business opportunities they create for local professionals.

9. Investigate the academic landscape in Africa, focusing on universities recognised in the QS World University Rankings 2024.

10. Explore the diverse programs offered by African universities and their implications for international students' personal and professional development.

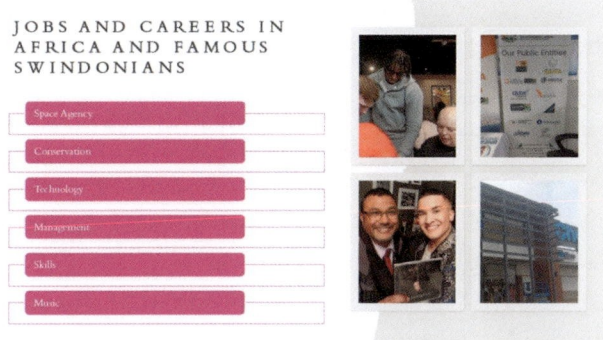

JOBS AND CAREERS IN AFRICA AND FAMOUS SWINDONIANS

Space Agency

Conservation

Technology

Management

Skills

Music

Cllr Dawn Denton and writer:" If you want to impact the world, write a book, get involved with your community, and be kind. You have knowledge, experience and ideas that the world needs. Whether you put it all on paper or stand up for your community by putting yourself forward as an elected councillor, you educate, inspire, and empower others. And that is being a kind, caring and community-driven human being. Be brave. Be bold. Be brilliant!"

Famous Africans who have made remarkable contributions to society, as per the BBC, include:

Aliko Dangote (Nigeria): Regarded as the richest black man in the world and Africa's wealthiest individual, Dangote possesses an impressive fortune estimated at $10.3 billion. His business ventures span various sectors, including cement, sugar, and oil, showcasing his substantial impact on Africa's economy and infrastructure development. His entrepreneurial spirit has reshaped industries and created countless job opportunities across the continent.

Elon Musk (South Africa): Often called the "Rocket Man," Musk is synonymous with innovation and cutting-edge technology. He is the visionary behind companies like Tesla, SpaceX, and X, working tirelessly to revolutionise transportation through electric vehicles that aim to reduce carbon emissions and combat climate change. His forward-thinking projects, such as developing urban transportation solutions using advanced technology and plans to establish a human colony on Mars, underscore his ambition to alter the fabric of human existence.

Koos Bekker (South Africa): A formidable figure in the media and entertainment landscape, Bekker is known as the "go-getter of Asia." As CEO of Naspers, he made a groundbreaking investment in the Chinese tech giant Tencent in 2001, committing $32 million of Naspers' capital. This strategic move has since skyrocketed in value to an impressive $116 billion, linking his company's fortunes to Tencent's success. Bekker's refusal to accept a traditional salary in favour of stock options illustrates his unwavering confidence in the company he leads.

According to https://www.globalcitizen.org/en/content/50-powerful-women-africa-forbes-magazine/, several influential African women have emerged as powerful leaders:

Graça Machel (South Africa and Mozambique): At 74, Machel is a towering figure in Africa. She is celebrated for her remarkable journey from education minister in Mozambique to an international advocate for women's rights and social justice. As minister from 1975 to 1989, her policies had a lasting impact on the country's education system, making her a pivotal force in shaping future generations.

Chimamanda Ngozi Adichie (Nigeria): This 40-year-old literary powerhouse has captivated audiences worldwide with her profound storytelling. Her acclaimed novels Purple Hibiscus and Half of a Yellow Sun explore themes of identity, post-colonialism, and the complexities of Nigerian society. Adichie's eloquence and powerful narratives have solidified her status as a leading voice in contemporary literature, inspiring readers around the globe.

Winnie Byanyima (Uganda): As the Executive Director of UNAIDS, Byanyima is a relentless advocate for global health and human rights. With a rich background that includes serving as a member of parliament and working with various international organisations, her leadership is pivotal in spearheading initiatives to combat HIV/AIDS, demonstrating a deep commitment to health equity and social justice.

Rebecca Enonchong (Cameroon): As the Founder and CEO of AppsTech, Enonchong has emerged as a significant figure in the African technology landscape. Her work focuses on empowering businesses through tailored technology solutions, and she is a prominent advocate for tech innovation across the continent, fostering an environment of entrepreneurship and growth.

Irene Charnley (South Africa): A dynamic business leader, Charnley founded Smile Communications, a telecommunications company that has transformed access to communication services across various regions. Her tenacity and commitment to enhancing connectivity have facilitated digital access for many.

Jennifer Riria (Kenya): As the Group CEO of Echo Network Africa and a founding member of the Kenya Women Finance Trust, Riria is a trailblazer in financial inclusivity. Her initiatives focus on empowering women through access to financial resources and support, fostering economic independence and growth for marginalised communities.

Louise Mushikiwabo (Rwanda): As the Secretary General of the Organisation Internationale de la Francophonie (OIF), Mushikiwabo champions cultural and linguistic diversity across nations. Her leadership is instrumental in promoting the French language and fostering cooperation among Francophone countries, encouraging dialogue and cultural exchange.

Charlize Theron (South Africa): A globally recognised Hollywood actor, Theron is known for her award-winning performances and commitment to philanthropy. Through her charitable foundation, she supports a range of causes, including women's rights and HIV/AIDS prevention, using her platform to advocate for critical social issues.

These individuals excel in their respective fields and serve as beacons of inspiration, driving change and empowering future generations worldwide.

Debate.

1. How would you address the concern that despite local grassroots efforts, systemic issues such as poverty and inequality may undermine the effectiveness of these initiatives in creating lasting change?

2. What would you say to someone who argues that collaboration with neighbourhood police watches may not fully engage or reflect the needs of the communities they aim to serve?

3. Have you considered the possibility that the resources devoted to grassroots projects might be better allocated to more extensive systemic programs that tackle the root causes of issues like knife crime and educational disparities?

CHAPTER 8: HOW TO PLAN A TRIP TO AFRICAN CITIES OR SWINDON, UK

If you have internet access, explore a range of travel websites, such as TUI, British Airways, Virgin Atlantic, Kenyan Airways, and South African Airways. These platforms offer valuable resources to help you plan your trip efficiently. Look for comprehensive details on routes to your chosen destination, compare prices for flights and accommodation, and discover different lodging options that fit your budget and preferences.

If your plans include working in Africa or Swindon, securing the correct visa or work permit is vital. Each country has specific requirements based on your nationality and the type of work you intend to do, whether short-term or long-term. It's advisable to gather precise information about the visa process directly from the embassy or consulate of the country where you plan to work. They will guide you on documentation, application procedures, and timelines.

Carstens shares: "I always believed South Africans would rise above difficult times to build a brighter future for everyone. Durban has always enchanted me with its wonderful people, stunning beaches, and exciting water sports, as well as with the PYC Yacht Club. In 1989, my late wife from Bulawayo, Zimbabwe, visited twice. We explored places like the Matopos and Victoria Falls. We took a memorable trip through Bulawayo and the Eastern Highlands to Great Zimbabwe and Kariba Dam on the Zambezi, where we camped by the lake. I could go on with countless stories about meeting my future partner, my great love, but I often wonder what interests' others and how to keep it brief. South Africa has provided me with so many tales! I've experienced incredible moments—from walking in Umfolozi with Rhinos, with a black Rhino surprisingly charging my car (in my beloved black Ford Fiesta XR2 from Germany), to hitchhiking in the Cape with snakes and a tent in Arniston. I once even climbed into a refrigeration unit in a van to reach Worcester Station. And I can't forget my 1985 trip to witness Halley's Comet from the Cave atop the Amphitheatre, a breathtaking 3400m up in the Drakensberg (I still have the slides!). Durban KZN holds many cherished memories for me, including visits to national parks and spots like Hole in the Wall and the St. Lucia Crocodile Research Centre, where Ranger Jeff Gaisford drove us up the beaches in his classic 60-year-old Land Rover toward Cape Vidal and other parks like Mkuzi, Umfolozi, Hluhluwe, and the Tongas Elephant Park..."

Virgin Atlantic presents the Sun City Resort as a premier vacation spot, often dubbed the "Las Vegas of Africa." This luxurious getaway provides a full range of experiences, featuring a bustling casino, two excellent golf courses, superb dining options, expansive water parks, and four stunning hotels, each with its unique offerings. Beyond its recreational activities, Sun City is conveniently located near some of South Africa's best wildlife attractions, such as Pilanesberg National Park, known for its rich biodiversity, the Madikwe Game Reserve, one of Africa's largest game reserves, and the Kwena Gardens Crocodile Sanctuary, where you can learn about and observe these fascinating reptiles up close.

Don't miss the vibrant capital city of Ghana, Accra, which welcomes over a million tourists each year, making it an essential stop on your travel itinerary. Whether you're reconnecting with loved ones or visiting for the first time, Accra boasts a lively community steeped in history and culture. One of its must-visit attractions is the National Museum of Ghana, which offers a profound exploration of the country's heritage through extensive collections that portray various aspects of African culture, daily life, and significant historical moments. To fully enrich your visit, consider joining a guided tour that will provide essential insights into the exhibits.

For an informative historical experience, visit the Kwame Nkrumah Memorial Park, dedicated to Ghana's first president and a pivotal figure in the nation's independence movement. This significant site features a striking mausoleum and a museum that meticulously chronicles Nkrumah's life, his role in Ghana's liberation, and the journey to independence. The exhibits reflect the rich legacy of Ghanaian leadership and the struggles faced in the fight for self-governance.

Be sure to explore additional resources and information at https://www.gov.uk/foreign-travel-advice/south-africa/entry-requirements. This comprehensive guide will help enhance your travel plans and ensure you make the most of your adventures in Africa. If you have internet access, take the opportunity to explore a range of travel websites such as TUI, British Airways, Virgin Atlantic, Kenyan Airways, and South African Airways. These platforms offer valuable resources to help you plan your trip efficiently. Look for comprehensive details on routes to your chosen destination, compare prices for flights and accommodations, and discover different lodging options that fit your budget and preferences.

If your plans include working in Africa or Swindon, securing the right visa or work permit is vital. Each country has specific requirements based on your nationality and the type of work you intend to do, whether short-term or long-term. It's advisable to gather precise information about the visa process directly from the embassy or consulate of the country where you plan to work. They will guide you on the necessary documentation, application procedures, and timelines.

Virgin Atlantic presents the Sun City Resort as a premier vacation spot, often dubbed the "Las Vegas of Africa." This luxurious getaway provides a full range of experiences, featuring a bustling casino, two excellent golf courses, superb dining options, expansive water parks, and four stunning hotels, each with its unique offerings. Beyond its recreational activities, Sun City is conveniently located near some of South Africa's best wildlife attractions, such as Pilanesberg National Park, known for its rich biodiversity, the Madikwe Game Reserve, one of Africa's largest game reserves, and the Kwena Gardens Crocodile Sanctuary, where you can learn about and observe these fascinating reptiles up close.

Don't miss the vibrant capital city of Ghana, Accra, which welcomes over a million tourists each year, making it an essential stop on your travel itinerary. Whether you're reconnecting with loved ones or visiting for the first time, Accra boasts a lively community steeped in history and culture. One of its must-visit attractions is the National Museum of Ghana, which offers a profound exploration of the country's heritage through extensive collections that portray various aspects of African culture, daily life, and significant historical moments. To fully enrich your visit, consider joining a guided tour that will provide essential insights into the exhibits.

For an informative historical experience, visit the Kwame Nkrumah Memorial Park, dedicated to Ghana's first president and a pivotal figure in the nation's independence movement. This significant site features a striking mausoleum and a museum that meticulously chronicles Nkrumah's life, his role in Ghana's liberation, and the journey to independence. The exhibits reflect the rich legacy of Ghanaian leadership and the struggles faced in the fight for self-governance.

Be sure to explore additional resources and information at https://www.gov.uk/foreign-travel-advice/south-africa/entry-requirements. This comprehensive guide will help enhance your travel plans and ensure you make the most of your adventures in Africa.

Hunt, a resident of Swindon, remarks: "Africa is an incredibly diverse continent, rich in its people and climates. It's best to view it as three distinct regions: Mediterranean Africa, enclosed by deserts and thriving river oases; Equatorial Africa, home to lush tropical forests; and Southern Africa, stretching from the Caprivi Strip through rugged landscapes to the tumultuous seas below."

Kristy shares her thoughts about Swindon: "Coate Water is a beautiful spot that caters to everyone, including those with disabilities. It features the famous diving board, a children's splash park, and crazy golf links nestled between Sir Jeffrey's Museum and the Spotted Cow, perfect for a light lunch in the sun. Coate Water boasts four lakes connected by Curley Bridge, offering miles of paths ideal for pushchairs, wheelchairs, and bike riders. During summer, there are great opportunities for barbecuing. From making daisy chains to spotting spring mushrooms, the area comes alive with snowdrops and wildflowers that attract various insects. Around Coate Water, you can find hidden birds by the lakes, showcasing the finest in wildlife. If you're lucky, you might even spot kingfishers or the rare roe deer. It's a fantastic place for photographers to pursue their passion while families enjoy the beauty of nature."

CHAPTER 9: SPORTS, MUSIC, ART, LITERATURE & EVENTS

Jane-nana always stands out with her diverse hairstyles and makeup choices. She believes that from the elaborate and eye-catching coiffures of the Himba people in Namibia to the modern braiding styles celebrated worldwide, African hair has transformed into a powerful symbol of cultural pride, personal identity, and societal resilience. These hairstyles reflect individual and collective identities and serve as a vibrant canvas for storytelling, a means of self-expression, and a crucial link to the continent's rich and diverse heritage.

When the author interacts with accomplished African ministers, they vividly emphasise the vastness and diversity of the world's second-largest continent. Stretching over an impressive 30 million square kilometres, Africa is a land of striking contrasts and breathtaking beauty, home to more than 1.5 billion people. This immense territory is divided into 54 distinct countries, each brimming with unique cultures, languages, and traditions. The continent boasts thousands of ethnic groups that intricately weave together a rich tapestry of cultural heritage.

LG: "If We dismantled Apartheid with the Support we received around the World, We could save The Curries Fountain Stadium in Durban; kindly assist me with Support from the UK… Remember that Curries Fountain Stadium was The Mecca for Non Racial Sports," a message to the international SAAn.

The rise of ancient civilisations deeply influences Africa's historical narrative, each leaving an indelible mark on the world. Imagine the magnificent pyramids of Egypt, a testament to human ingenuity that glows in the sunlight, or the enchanting lands of Nubia, known for their vibrant history and artistry. The remarkable kingdom of Axum, famed for its monumental obelisks, once served as a thriving hub of commerce and culture. Great Zimbabwe, with its impressive stone ruins, echoes the legacy of a powerful civilisation that engaged in trade across vast distances. Meanwhile, the sophisticated Mali Empire flourished as a centre of learning, trade, and cultural creativity, making substantial contributions to advancing human knowledge and artistic expression. Together, these historical gems not only define Africa's past but continue to illuminate its vibrant present.

Africa's cultural richness is significantly enhanced by its impact on the global stage, particularly through the African diaspora. This community has been instrumental in preserving, adapting, and transforming African traditions across various regions worldwide. As a result, African heritage not only survives but continues to flourish and evolve in diverse contexts.

Central to African cultural practices are the instruments of rhythm—drums, traditional music, and vibrant dances. Musical genres such as Afrobeat, Highlife, and Gqom have become internationally recognized and celebrated, ensuring that African rhythms resonate across continents. More recently, genres like Amapiano and Afrobeats have gained immense popularity, finding their way into the playlists of numerous Western artists and highlighting the global reach of African music.

Sports are another area where Africa shines prominently on the world stage. South Africa, in particular, has established itself as a powerhouse in various athletic disciplines, routinely producing world champions in rugby, football (soccer), netball, and cricket. Notable football clubs such as Kaizer Chiefs and Orlando Pirates have become symbols of excellence in the sport, while the Sharks Rugby Club adds to the country's impressive sports legacy.

For those looking to engage with Africa's lively events and cultural celebrations, important upcoming activities can be found at: https://www.facebook.com/groups/400007548096533/?ref=share.

South Africa's successful hosting of the 2010 FIFA World Cup was a historic milestone, showcasing not only the nation's capacity to organize major global sporting events but also its passion for football. Meanwhile, Kenya and Ethiopia have cemented their reputation as dominant forces in long-distance running, with athletes from these countries frequently excelling in international competitions. South Africa has also welcomed the world for the Rugby World Cup in 1995 and the Cricket World Cup in 2003, events that have brought immense pride and recognition to the continent.

Furthermore, Africa has successfully hosted six editions of the Pan Arab Games and five of the Mediterranean Games, showcasing its ability to unite and celebrate athleticism. It is worth noting that Durban was chosen to be the host city for the 2022 Commonwealth Games in 2015 but unfortunately lost its status as host city in 2017, highlighting the challenges that often accompany large-scale events.

Prominent continental tournaments such as the African Games, the Africa Cup of Nations, the CAF Champions League, the African Championships in Athletics, the African Rally Championship, and the Sunshine Tour demonstrate not only Africa's commitment to sports and competition but also its capacity to produce world-class athletes and unforgettable sporting events. Each tournament is a testament to Africa's dynamic and competitive spirit, emphasizing the continent's rich cultural and athletic legacy.

Further work.

1. Explore the cultural significance of hairstyles among the Himba people in Namibia, focusing on traditional practices and meanings.

2. Research the history of African hairstyles across different regions and ethnic groups to understand their evolution and diversity.

3. Investigate the role of hairstyles in expressing personal and communal identities within African communities.

4. Analyze the symbolism of hairstyles as a medium for storytelling and cultural heritage.

5. Examine the impact of the African diaspora on the adaptation and transformation of African hairstyles globally.

6. Gather examples of notable African braiding styles and their variations in different countries.

7. Study contemporary movements related to African hair, including discussions about natural hair, beauty standards, and societal resistance.

8. Investigate the influence of African hairstyles in global fashion and popular culture, including their representation in media.

9. Reference scholarly articles and books on African cultural practices, focusing on hair and identity to support arguments.

10. Compile a list of relevant online resources and community voices discussing the significance of African hair and hairstyles.

CHAPTER 10: BUSINESS AND CHARITY: ISSUES & SOLUTIONS FOR COMMUNITIES

Vineshree speaks passionately about the South African Association: "In South Africa, our initiatives are vibrant and impactful, aimed at fostering sustainable societal change. We actively support football programs that nurture young talent and encourage community involvement. Additionally, we are at the forefront of essential anti-gender-based violence initiatives led by Suraya, who diligently works to educate and empower individuals to address and tackle these pressing issues.

Moreover, we are taking significant steps to curb crime within our communities through strategic projects spearheaded by Jimmy, who is dedicated to creating safer spaces for everyone. Our commitment extends to providing vital tuition support for disadvantaged students, ensuring they have access to quality education. Nolan plays a crucial role in this mission, assisting visually impaired individuals by equipping them with the tools and resources necessary for academic and life success.

Dawn is leading our book publishing efforts, advocating for literature that inspires and educates. Beyond these initiatives, we are engaged in a variety of exciting projects that foster meaningful change across different sectors of society.

We wholeheartedly encourage you to get involved and take action in our efforts. As Gandhi wisely said, "Be the change you seek." The South African Association proudly supports Fatima's campaign—learn more about our mission at Fatimascampaign.com. We are passionate advocates for The Power of Movement, promoting empowered hashtags such as #loveandpeace, #FOLLOWFATIMA, #changeiscoming, and #CHILDRENAREOURFUTURE to raise awareness and inspire collective action.

Additionally, we stand united in support of Nic Careem's impactful initiative, "Inspiring Young Voices." This campaign features the "Letter to Mandela" competition, motivating young people to share their thoughts on leadership, resilience, and social justice.

Nic:"Recently, I had the privilege of meeting my distinguished friend, His Excellency Jeremiah Nyamane Mamabolo, the South African High Commissioner to the UK. Together, we are committed to making a significant impact in our communities and shaping a brighter, more equitable future for generations to come."

There are many questions yet to be answered.

1. How would you address those who argue that while your initiatives are admirable, the scale and resources committed may fall short in creating lasting change within such a complex

societal landscape?

2. Have you thought about the viewpoint that the effectiveness of football programs might be limited if they do not tackle the deeper socio-economic issues facing South African youth?

3. What would you say to someone who believes that focusing on individual initiatives like Suraya's or Jimmy's might overlook the necessity for a more comprehensive and systemic approach to combat gender-based violence and crime?

BAZIL SOLOMON

BUSINESS AND CHARITY

| Liberty Life | Nolan Blind Support Charity | South African Association |
| Trish Nails | Jane Rodbourne Hairstyles | The South African Spaza shop |

CHAPTER 11:
CONTACTS AND
QUESTIONS

Join the south African association on Facebook

https://www.facebook.com/share/14ng8jYhbo/

Email bazil.solomon@gmail.com

CHAPTER 12: ACKNOWLEDGEMENTS AND REFERENCES

1. Agawu, K., 2014. Representing African music: Postcolonial notes, queries, positions. Routledge.
2. Alcorn, M., 1987. Top Caribbean texts for GCSE.
3. Boadi, C., 2021. An Investigation of how Cultural Dimensions Influence Students' Achievements in Secondary Schools in London (Doctoral dissertation, University of Roehampton).
4. Bush, R., 1987. GCSE literature and multicultural concerns. Wasafiri
5. Busia, K.A., 2023. The challenge of Africa. Routledge.
6. Das, M.B. and Espinoza, S.A., 2019. Inclusion matters in Africa. World Bank Group.
7. Davenport, T. and Saunders, C., 2000. South Africa: A modern history. Springer.
8. Davidson, B., 2013. Africa in history. Hachette UK.
9. Defo, B.K., 2014. Demographic, epidemiological, and health transitions: are they relevant to population health patterns in Africa?. Global health action.
10. Demie, F. and McLean, C., 2007. Raising the achievement of African heritage pupils: a case study of good practice in British schools. Educational Studies

11. Demie, F., 2021. The educational achievement of Black African children in England.
12. Durban, B. and Cowling, L., 2005. ABOUT SOUTH AFRICA. Global Entertainment Media: Content, Audiences, Issues,
13. Essex, J., Alexiadou, N. and Zwozdiak-Myers, P., 2021. Understanding inclusion in teacher education–a view from student teachers in England. International Journal of Inclusive Education, 25(12), pp.1425-1442.
14. Martin, P.M. and O'meara, P. eds., 1995. Africa. Indiana University Press.
15. Miller, J.C., 1999. History and Africa/Africa and history. The American Historical Review
16. Mudimbe, V.Y., 1988. The invention of Africa: Gnosis, philosophy, and the order of knowledge.
17. Norwich, B.R.A.H.M., 2012. How inclusion policy works in the UK (England): Successes and issues. What works in inclusion
18. Nzongola-Ntalaja, G., 2013. The Congo from Leopold to Kabila: a people's history. Bloomsbury Publishing.
19. Osler, A. and Morrison, M., 2002. Can race equality be inspected? Challenges for policy and practice raised by the OFSTED school inspection framework. British Educational Research Journal, 28(3), pp.327-338.
20. Richmond, R.C., 2013. Inclusive schools, the quality of education and OFSTED school inspection. In Special educational provision in the context of inclusion. David Fulton Publishers.
21. Rowles, N., 2020. GCSE 9-1 Geography AQA Exam Practice: Grades 4-6. Oxford University Press-Children.
22. Sayed, Y. and Kanjee, A., 2013. Assessment in Sub-Saharan Africa: challenges and prospects. Assessment in Education: Principles, Policy & Practice, 20(4), pp.373-384.
23. Spaull, N., 2011. A preliminary analysis of SACMEQ III

South Africa. Stellenbosch: Stellenbosch University.

24. Strand, S., 2006. The educational progress of African heritage pupils in all Lambeth schools. Demie, F., McLean, C., & Lewis, K.(2006)(Eds). The achievement of African heritage pupils: Good practice in Lambeth schools. Lambeth: Lambeth Children and Young People's Service.

25. Walton, E., 2011. Getting inclusion right in South Africa. Intervention in school and clinic, 46(4), pp.240-245.

26. 1860 Heritage

27. Ant-apartheid Museum

28. Black Southwest Network UK

29. Carstens L

30. CFoSA

31. Cllr Dawn Denton

32. DAAbroadUK

33. Dr Saths Cooper

34. Dr Sharon Jacob

35. Dr Stuart Whigham

36. Fatima Whitbread OBE

37. Football Association FA Swindon and Wiltshire

38. Friends and family colleagues

39. Grammarly AI

40. Jane Norgrove

41. Joy, Patricia and Nancy

42. Kharina Secondary School

43. Liden Library and Community Hub

44. My dear wife, Sharon and daughter Amelie.

45. Nana Mthembu

46. Nelson Mandela Foundation

47. Nic Careem

48. Nolan

49. Northlands Primary School

50. Open University
51. Oxford Brookes University
52. Oxford University
53. South African Association and Members
54. South African Indian Veterans
55. Swindon Borough Council
56. Swindon Town Football Club STFC
57. Trish Rawlins
58. University of South Africa UNISA
59. Witswaterand University

"An incredible story of Africa, vibrant cultures, breathtaking landscapes, and dynamic communities which coexist alongside urbanisation and economic change challenges. With its storied history and diverse population, the United Kingdom presents a unique blend of tradition and innovation. The book can help students, scholars and the general public in the UK & Africa and globally reflect on how you can actively contribute to positive change amidst your daily struggles and trials and tribulations is vital. It can help you embrace the opportunity to make an impact and transform your circumstances into something meaningful!": South African Association.

"A great book to begin your journey in understanding modern Africa & UK": Dr Sharon Jacob

An accomplished author, Bazil Solomon BA, PGCE, MSc, MPhil has brought over 30 years of diverse experience across various fields, including information technology, education, politics, and community activism. His extensive body of work has significantly impacted, particularly in academic circles, where he delves into a wide range of essential subjects. He passionately explores the complexities of artificial intelligence, the nuances of social media collaborative work—a concept he innovatively introduced as SMCW—and the intricacies of linguistics. Furthermore, his writings address pressing issues such as diabetes management, the principles of democracy, and the essential concepts of equality, diversity, and inclusion (EDI). Bazil also actively engages with his audience through vibrant social media platforms, where he discusses various community-related topics, fostering dialogue and inspiring action.

Printed in Great Britain
by Amazon

57963882R00037